HEINEMANN HISTORY

THE ROMAN EMPIRE

STUDY UNITS

D1635486

HEINEMANN EDUCATION

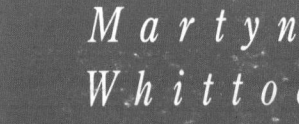

A26119

Martyn Whittock

Heinemann Educational,
a division of Heinemann Educational Books Ltd,
Halley Court, Jordan Hill, Oxford OX2 8EJ

OXFORD LONDON EDINBURGH MADRID
ATHENS BOLOGNA PARIS MELBOURNE
SYDNEY AUCKLAND SINGAPORE TOKYO
IBADAN NAIROBI HARARE GABORONE
PORTSMOUTH NH (USA)

First published 1991

British Library Cataloguing in Publication Data
Whittock, Martyn J. (Martyn John)
The Roman Empire.
1. Rome (Italy), history, B.C.27 – A.D. 476
I. Title
937.06

ISBN 0-435-31274-X

Designed by Ron Kamen, Green Door Design Ltd,
Basingstoke
Illustrated by Jeff Edwards Douglas Hall
Stuart Hughes Terry Thomas

Printed in Spain by Mateo Cromo

Acknowledgements

The author and publisher would like to thank the following for permission to reproduce photographs:

Ancient Art & Architecture Collection: 3.3A, 4.2A
Archäologisches Landesmuseum, Schleswig: 4.1A
Archivio Moro, Rome: 4.6A
Ashmolean Museum: 1.1F
Bibliothèque Nationale: 4.3E
The Trustees of the British Museum: 1.2D, 2.1B, 2.2B, 2.4B, 2.5A, 2.9A, 2.9B, 3.12A, D and E, 4.2C, 4.4A
Simon Chapman: 4.6C
Committee for Aerial Photography, Cambridge: p25
C. M. Dixon: Front cover, 1.2E, 2.1C, 2.3A and C, 2.6E, 3.3C, 3.4B, 3.5B and C, 3.7A, C and D, 3.8A, 3.10A, 3.11A and C, 4.1C
Sonia Halliday Photographs: 2.2C, 2.4C, 3.5A, 3.8B, 3.8D (E, H. C. Birch), 4.5A and B
Michael Holford: 1.1A, 1.1D, 3.5B, 3.9C, 3.11D
Israel Museum, Jerusalem: 1.2C
Lion Publishing plc/David Townsend: 1.2A
Mansell Collection: p25
Alan Millard: 1.1E
Museum of London: 4.4F
The National Gallery: 4.6B
National Museum of Ireland: 4.1D
Nationalmuseet, Copenhagen: 3.2G
Dr P. J. Reynolds/Butser Ancient Farm: 3.9D
Rheinisches Landesmuseum, Trier: 3.5A, 3.10B and C
Chris Ridgers: 4.6D
Römisch-Germanisches Museum: 2.9D
Tyne & Wear Museum Service: 3.1D
Vatican Museum: 2.1A

Roger Wood: 3.8C
Woodmansterne Picture Library/Museum of London: 3.9A

We are also grateful to the following for permission to reproduce copyright material:

Andromeda Oxford Ltd for Source 3.7B, taken from *Atlas of the Roman World* by Tim Cornell and John Matthews, Phaidon Press, 1982; B. T. Batsford Ltd for Source 1.2B, taken from *England Before Domesday* by Martin Jones; Longman Group UK Ltd for Source 1.3A, taken from *The Romans in Britain* by Dorothy Morrison, 1978.

Every effort has been made to contact copyright holders of material reproduced in this book. Any omissions will be rectified in subsequent printings if notice is given to the publisher.

Details of Written Sources

In some sources the wording or sentence structure has been simplified to ensure that the source is accessible.

The Anglo-Saxon Chronicle (Trans. G. N. Garmonsway), J. M. Dent and Sons Ltd, 1953: 4.4C
Saint Augustine, *City of God* (Ed. David Knowles), Penguin, 1972: 4.2B
D. Breeze and B. Dobson, *Hadrian's Wall*, Allen Lane, 1976: 2.6B
Julius Caesar, *Commentaries* (Ed. R. L. A. Du Pontet), Oxford University Press, 1900: 2.7A
Simon Esmonde Cleary, *The Ending of Roman Britain*, Barnes and Noble Books, 1989: 4.4E
Tim Cornell and John Matthews, *Atlas of the Roman World*, Phaidon Press, 1982: 2.1D, 2.2A, 2.5B, 3.2F, 3.4C
K. Greene, *Archaeology of the Roman Economy*, Batsford, 1986: 3.4D
Good News Bible, Collins, 1976: 3.1A
Catherine Hills, *Blood of the British from Ice Age to Norman Conquest*, George Philip in association with Channel 4 TV company, 1986: 4.3D
J. Liversidge, *Roman Britain*, Longman, 1958: 2.8A
A. Millard, *Discoverers from the Time of Jesus*, Lion, 1990: 2.3B, 2.9E, 3.11B, 3.12B and C
R. W. Moore, *The Roman Commonwealth*, English Universities Press, 1942: 3.3D
Oxford Dictionary of Quotations, Oxford University Press, 1982: 1.1C
J. Percival, *The Roman Villa: a Historical Introduction*, Batsford, 1976: 4.1B, 4.3B and C
Michael Postan, *The Medieval Economy and Society*, Weidenfeld and Nicolson, 1972: 4.4G
J. M. Roberts, *History of the World*, Penguin, 1980: 2.6A and C, 4.5C
R. R. Sellman, *Roman Britain*, Methuen, 1956: 2.8B
Diodorus Siculus, *Library of History* (Trans. C. H. Oldfather), Heinemann, 1939: 2.7B
P. Salway, *Roman Britain*, Oxford University Press, 1981: 2.5E, 2.6D, 2.8C, 2.9CL.
A. Thompson, *Romans and Blacks*, Routledge, 1989: 3.2A, B, C and E
G. M. Trevelyan, *History of England*, Longman, 1926: 4.4D

91 92 93 94 95   11 10 9 8 7 6 5

CONTENTS

1.1 Words from the Past

Historians use **primary sources** to find out about the past. Primary sources come from the time the historian is studying. They become **evidence** when they are used to support a statement. For example, Source A is evidence for the statement that 'Vilbia was a Roman name'. Some primary sources are written down. Many different kinds of written sources have survived from Roman times. For example, words carved on buildings, poems and descriptions of people and places. Some of them are official records and lists of who should pay tax. Some were meant for lots of people to read, others were meant to be kept secret. Often the words were written in Latin. This was the official language of the Roman Empire, although other languages were also used.

A

SOURCE

A curse written in Latin on a piece of lead. It reads: 'He who stole Vilbia from me, may he waste away like water'.

When an historian reads a primary source, he or she needs to ask certain questions about it:
- When was it written?
- Who wrote it?
- Why was it written?
- Where did the writer get the information from?
- Has it survived as it was written, or has it been copied?
- If it has been copied, could mistakes have been made?

If a number of copies of a written source survive, they can be compared to see if they tell the same story. Sometimes, though, only very few have survived. This makes it harder to be sure that what happened is exactly as it was written.

There are some 'words from the past' in this Unit. They are written primary sources from Roman times.

B

SOURCE

It is impossible for a man to live there for half an hour, but vipers and many snakes and all other kinds of wild beasts live there, and strangest of all, the natives say that if a man crosses the wall he immediately dies, unable to stand the poisonous air. Wild beasts that go there die too!

A description of northern Britain written in the 6th century AD by Procopius.

C

SOURCE

In our orchard I saw you picking
Dewy apples with your mother....
How I saw you!
How I fell in love!

A poem written to a girl by Virgil, a man who lived from 70–19 BC.

D

SOURCE

A carved stone found on Hadrian's Wall. It dates from about AD 142. It is written in Latin. It reads: 'A detachment of the Twentieth Legion of Valeria and Victrix made this'.

E

SOURCE

Greek writing on a piece of pot from Egypt. It says that a man, named Pekysis, paid his taxes on 12 July, AD 144. He paid 16 silver coins.

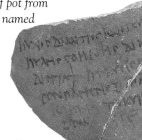

F

SOURCE

Writing in a book made from wooden boards. This was found in Egypt and dates from the 1st century AD. It is written in Greek.

Activities...

1 Explain what a primary source is, in your own words.

2 Give three examples of the types of written primary sources which may survive from Roman times.

3 a What questions does an historian have to ask about written primary sources?
b Which is the most important question to ask? Explain your answer.

4 Can you think of five written primary sources which would be useful to an historian studying life in your school? Say why each of them would be useful.

5 Which of the sources in this Unit could an historian use to find out about the personal feelings of people in the past?

6 In what ways could Sources D and E be useful to an historian?

7 Look carefully at Sources A, D, E and F. Why would you find it difficult to read the information written on these sources?

8 How can you tell from Source B that Procopius never visited northern Britain?

1.2 Pieces of the Past

A

SOURCE

◀ *Remains of a house in Jerusalem. It was burnt in AD 70, when the city was captured by a Roman army.*

Not all primary sources are written down. There are many different types of **non-written** primary sources. Many of these sources have survived from the Roman Empire. Some of them are big, like buildings. Others are small, like coins and tools. They might have been precious objects to the people using them or just ordinary, everyday things. All of these things can tell us about life in the past.

Some sources have been found by accident, others have been carefully searched for. **Archaeologists** are people who study remains from under the ground. They dig into the ground to find these remains. This is called an **excavation**. Here are some different sources which come from the time of the Roman Empire.

B

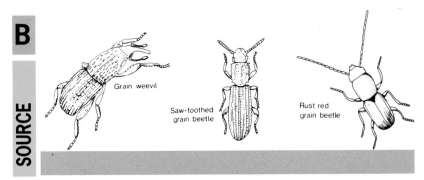

Grain weevil

Saw-toothed grain beetle

Rust red grain beetle

SOURCE

Insects discovered by archaeologists in a Roman building in York, England.

C

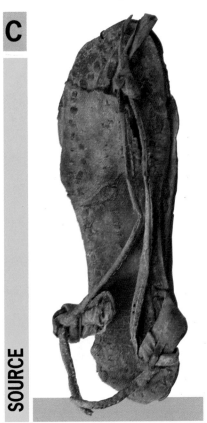

SOURCE

Sandal from Masada, in Israel. From about AD 74.

D SOURCE

Silver bowl from Mildenhall, England. It was probably buried in about AD 360, *to protect it from robbers.*

Activities...

1 a Why might an archaeologist decide to do an excavation?

2 a How might objects under the ground be found by accident? Think of as many ways as you can.
   b What five objects of yours could help archaeologists to learn about your life? What would each object tell them?

3 a Look at Source A and describe what you can see.
   b What else would you need to know about this house, in order to describe life in it?

4 Look at Sources B, C, D and E. What information does each source give to an historian?

E SOURCE

◀ *Picture of a woman holding a pen and writing tablet. This is from Pompeii, in Italy. It dates from the 1st century* AD.

1.3 Secondary Sources

Secondary sources usually come from later than the time being studied, and they are always **based on other sources**. Once historians have studied primary sources, they write down what they have learned about the past. What they write down is a secondary source.

Books written by historians do not always agree. Historians may have used different primary sources. They may have understood them differently. You must remember this when you read a history book. These different ways of understanding the sources are called **opinions**. Sometimes the people who wrote the primary sources had different opinions, too. Historians must decide which opinions are best supported by the evidence.

Not all secondary sources are written down. If someone draws a picture of what life was like in Roman times or builds a model of a Roman town, these would also be secondary sources.

The written sources in this Unit tell you about life in Britain before the Romans came, and how it changed when Britain became part of the Empire. They do not all agree with one another! Look at them very carefully.

B **SOURCE**
Because the Romans were clever and hardworking, and did most things better than the Britons, they soon ruled over all the land.

R. J. Unstead, 'Cavemen to Vikings', 1953.

C **SOURCE**
The condition of the people improved. Peace brought prosperity, a busy trade sprang up. Along with this corn trade came progress in the mining of tin, lead and copper and the making of weapons and dyeing and pottery.

G. T. Warner and C. Marten, 'Roman Britain', 1923.

An artist's impression of how people lived in Britain before the Romans invaded. From Dorothy Morrison, 'The Romans in Britain', 1978.

A **SOURCE**

D **SOURCE**

Technically, Roman Britons were able to produce good quality pottery, and a much wider range of iron tools. Farming benefited from the introduction of tools and equipment which enabled more heavily forested land to be cleared.

J. Wacher, 'Roman Britain', 1978.

E **SOURCE**

The tribes of the south-east of England [before the Romans arrived] were skillful farmers, artistic metal workers and well organized. Their rulers must have lived in a degree of comfort. On the whole, the country was peaceful and prosperous.

R. Collingwood, 'Roman Britain', 1923.

F **SOURCE**

For much of rural Britain the Roman invasion of AD 43 meant little change. In Wessex and the South Downs life continued much as before.

S. Woodell, 'The English Landscape', 1985.

G **SOURCE**

By the late Iron Age, lowland Britain was covered with villages, hamlets and farms. This pattern was changed a little during the Roman period but it remained substantially the same. Many Iron Age communities passed unaltered into the Roman period.

T. Rowley, 'Villages in the Landscape', 1987.

Activities...

1 Events in history sometimes take place for different reasons. These are called **causes**. Events in history often make other things happen. These are called **consequences**. Read Sources C and D. They both say that a consequence of Britain becoming part of the Roman Empire was that life improved for the people living in Britain.
   a Give one improvement mentioned in both sources.
   b Give one improvement mentioned only in Source C, and one improvement mentioned only in Source D.

2 **a** Read Source B. According to this writer, why did the Romans beat the Britons?
   b The writer of Source B gives no evidence to back up his opinion. Does this make it more or less likely that you will agree with him? Explain the reasons for your answer.

3 What primary sources might the historian have used as evidence for Source A?

4 Study Sources D, E, and F. For each complete the following table:

Source	Agrees or disagrees with B, C or D	Reason
E	Disagrees	E says tribes before the Romans were skillful and well organized. A makes them look hopeless compared with the Romans.

2.1 Roman Rise to Power

According to a Roman legend, the city of Rome was begun in 753 BC. The legend says that its founder was a man named Romulus. He and his brother Remus had been brought up by a wolf! This is a story. Its aim was probably to show how special the city of Rome was. A later legend said that Romulus was the son of Mars, the Roman god of war.

Archaeologists have discovered that, by the 6th century BC, there were a number of important regions in Italy. One of these was Etruria, where the **Etruscan** people lived. They were skilled in metalwork, land drainage, trading, building and road making. An Etruscan (Tarquin II) had made himself King of Rome, a town beside the river Tiber. It was sited at a place where the river could be crossed by a bridge. Ships could also reach Rome from the Mediterranean sea.

In 509 BC, a number of wealthy Roman families forced the king to leave the city. Rome became a **Republic** (a place ruled without a king or a queen). Rome began to grow in importance. Other cities were captured. Their rulers were allowed to keep their power as long as they supplied men for the Roman army and stayed loyal to Rome. This army made Rome strong.

In 390 BC, Rome was attacked and looted by tribes from Gaul (now France). Despite this, the Romans recovered. Then, in three brutal wars, they defeated the tribes from the Italian hills. Between 280 and 275 BC they fought the Greek king, Pyrrhus. He had been helping the Greek settlers, living in Italy, to resist the Romans. By 265 BC, most of southern Italy was controlled by Rome.

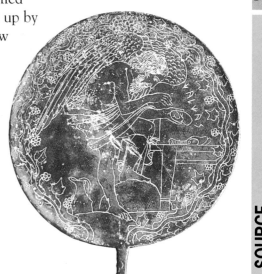

SOURCE A

A mirror made by an Etruscan metalworker. It shows a person telling the future by looking at an animal's intestines.

Early Rome and its neighbours

Land controlled by Greek settlers

→ Invasion by Gauls, 390 BC

GAUL

Etruria
Rome

ITALY

Mediterranean Sea

GREECE

| 0 | km | 500 |
| 0 | miles | 500 |

A Roman coin, made in 96 BC. It celebrates a Roman victory over Italian tribes at the battle of Lake Regillus. This took place in 499 BC. The Roman gods, Castor and Pollux, are shown on the coin. The Romans believed that these gods helped them to win the battle. They believed that after the battle, the gods watered their horses at Rome. This coin shows this scene.

D SOURCE

Tell me, all you who have journeyed through many lands, have you seen a more richly farmed land than Italy?

The Roman writer Varro, who lived in the 1st century BC.

C SOURCE

◄ *A statue of Romulus and Remus from the city of Rome.*

Activities...

1 **a** Make a timeline to show some of the important dates in early Roman history. Mark down all the dates mentioned in this Unit.

    b Mark on your timeline the point when you think Rome began to be powerful. Write a short paragraph explaining your choice.

2 **a** Look at Source D. According to Varro, what was special about Italy?

    b From the other information in this Unit, can you think of two other reasons why Rome was so successful?

3 Look at Source B, and its description. How useful would this be as evidence for what actually happened at the battle of Lake Regillus? Give reasons for your answer.

4 How could an historian use Sources A, B and C as evidence concerning the beliefs of the Romans and Etruscans?

5 What skills did the Etruscans have? Why would the Romans have found them useful?

2.2 Rivals for Trade

As Rome became more powerful, it was able to control what was bought and sold in Italy. This buying and selling of goods is called **trade**. The Romans found they had **trading rivals**. These were other people who wanted to buy and sell things in Italy. Greek traders had set up cities in Italy and Sicily. Tarentum and Syracuse were two important Greek cities in Italy. Soon they were at war with Rome.

In north Africa there was another great trading city, called **Carthage**. Its people were skilled sailors and shipbuilders. Rome and Carthage were soon rivals. Between 264 and 241 BC the rivalry turned into warfare. The Romans built their first navy to fight the Carthaginian fleet. The Romans captured the island of Sicily and it became the first Roman **province**, in 241 BC. A province was a foreign land captured and ruled by the Romans.

The Carthaginians tried to make up for the loss of Sicily. They captured territory in Spain. From 218–201 BC, a second war was fought with Rome. The Carthaginians were led by a skilled general, **Hannibal**. He led an army across the Alps and into Italy. He defeated the Romans at the Battles of Lake Trasimene and Cannae. Despite this, Rome survived. The towns of central Italy stayed loyal to Rome. The Roman general, Fabius Maximus, avoided any more great battles. Hannibal was not able to capture Rome itself. Soon he was running short of supplies.

The Romans struck back. They attacked the Carthaginian cities in Spain. The Roman army crossed to Africa to threaten Carthage. Hannibal was forced to leave Italy. He went to defend Carthage itself. In 202 BC, he was defeated at the Battle of Zama. In 150 BC a third war broke out. This time the Romans were determined to take no chances. In 146 BC, they totally destroyed the city of Carthage. A new Roman city was built nearby.

A

SOURCE

The Carthaginians will not injure the people of any other city of the Latins who are subjects [under the control] of Rome. As far as the Latins who are not subjects, they shall keep their hands off their cities, and if they take any such city they shall hand it over to the Romans unharmed. They shall build no forts in Latin territories.

Treaty between Rome and Carthage in 201 BC.

Activities...

1
  a Why were Rome and Carthage rivals?

  b Give one way in which the war with Carthage made the Romans try out new ways of fighting.

  c Give five reasons why Hannibal failed to win the war in Italy.

2 Most of our primary sources for the war with Carthage were written by Romans.

  a How trustworthy do you think these would be as evidence?

  b Would they be good, or bad things for historians to use if they wanted to find out about this war? Explain the reasons behind your answer.

3
  a Source B celebrates a Roman victory. How many years were there between this victory and when the coin was made? What does this tell you about the importance of this victory to the Romans?

  b Read Source A. Make a list in your own words of the things that this treaty stopped the Carthaginians from doing.

  c How useful would you find Source C, if you tried to find out what the city of Carthage was like before 146 BC? Give reasons for your answer.

Roman coin from 125 BC. It celebrates the Roman victory over Carthage, at the battle of Panormus. This battle was fought in 251 BC. In this battle the Romans captured over 100 Carthaginian war elephants.

The site of the Roman city of Carthage.

Trade routes at the time of the wars with Carthage

— Trade routes between Greek cities
— Trade routes between Carthaginian cities

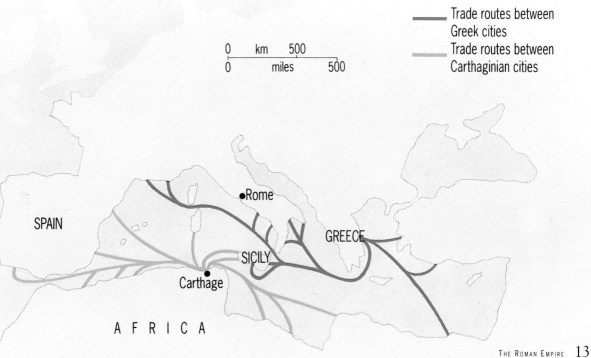

2.3 The Roman Army

One of the reasons for Rome's success was its army. As Roman power grew, more people were made to join the army. At first the soldiers were the better-off citizens. They copied Greek armies and fought on foot with long spears. To begin with, they were sent home when a war ended. These part-time soliders paid for their own weapons and armour.

As the Roman Empire grew, the army had to fight further away from home. Being a soldier became a full-time job. They were no longer sent home at the end of the fighting. These full-time soldiers were well trained and disciplined. They had to be tough and confident in the use of a number of weapons.

Roman soldiers were grouped into large numbers called **legions**. Each legion was made up of 5,000 heavily armed foot soldiers and some cavalry. The legion included engineers, surveyors, stone masons and carpenters, as well as other craftsmen. As well as fighting major battles, the legions built forts, bridges and roads. When they were on a campaign, they built a camp fortified with banks and ditches at the end of each day's march.

The Jewish historian Josephus describing the siege of Gamla, AD 70.

A SOURCE

◀ *Roman legionaries building a fort. The campaigns of the Emperor Trajan (who ruled between AD 98 and 117) are shown on a massive column known as Trajan's Column. This is one of the scenes.*

They trained regularly. At Cawthorne in Yorkshire, they built practice camps where they trained in attacking forts held by the enemy. Only citizens of the Empire could join the legions. They joined for 25 years. When they retired they were given money (three gold coins) and land to farm.

Most of the actual fighting was done by soldiers called **auxiliaries**. They were not citizens of the Empire. They were made citizens when they retired. They included cavalry from Spain and Hungary and archers from the Middle East.

After about AD 100, the Empire stopped growing. The army then spent most of its time keeping hold of the lands that it had captured. This took a lot of men. More and more non-citizens were recruited as auxiliaries to defend the forts on the borders of the Empire.

Tribespeople, from outside the Empire, were also employed. They were put in regiments called **numeri**. Like the auxiliaries, the numeri often defended forts on the frontiers. They were not made citizens when they retired.

D SOURCE

They make a desert and call it 'peace'.

The Roman historian Tacitus, writing in about AD 90. He is describing how the Roman army treated the lands of the enemies of Rome.

Activities...

1 In what ways did the Roman army change after AD 100?

2 **a** Look at Sources A and C. What different views do they give of life in the Roman army?
  b If historians only had one of these sources, how would it affect their views of what Roman soldiers did for a living?

3 Look carefully at Source C. How did the Roman stonemason make the emperor look different from the ordinary soldiers?

4 Does Source D give a good or a bad impression of the Roman army?

5 Design a recruiting poster for the Roman legions. Describe a soldier's work, the skills he would need and the benefits of being in the Roman army.

C SOURCE

◄ A Roman emperor speaking to his soldiers, as shown on the Arch of Constantine.

2.4 The Roman Republic

When the last king had been overthrown in 509 BC, Rome became a republic. Power was held by a number of rich families. They met together in the **senate** and were called **senators**. The senate was the main law making group in Rome.

Each year, two senators were elected as **consuls** to run the city. These consuls were elected by a meeting of all the citizens. The voting was arranged so that the rich had more say than the poor in the elections. The consuls were advised by the members of the senate. In an emergency, the two consuls chose one man to be a **dictator** for six months. A dictator had a lot of power. All of these people were men. Women were not allowed to take part.

Other men were elected as **magistrates**. Some helped the consuls. Each year they carried out a census. Some organized sacrifices to the gods of Rome. This kind of government made Rome well organized. However, there was often rivalry between the wealthy families. These families were supported by their followers or **clients**. Rivalry could lead to violence.

Many poorer citizens, called **plebeians**, were not happy. They did not own much land and were often in debt. There was rivalry between the plebeians and the rich members of the senate. In 450 BC, plebeians took action to have Roman laws properly written down. These were called **The Twelve Tables**. The plebeians had two main ways of putting pressure on the wealthy people in Rome. They could refuse to fight in the army and they could threaten to leave Rome and set up their own city. These threats sometimes made the wealthy pay attention to the demands of the plebeians. In 492 BC, some plebeians were appointed as **tribunes**. These men had the power to defend the plebeians from injustice. However, Rome was mainly under the control of the rich. In time, though, some of these were wealthier plebeians.

A

SOURCE

The letters 'SPQR' stand for 'Senate and People of Rome'. These letters were put on buildings and on army standards. They helped explain who ran the government of Rome. These letters are from a modern draincover in the city of Rome.

B

SOURCE

A Roman copper coin made in AD 23. The letters show that it was made 'By permission of the senate'.

Activities...

1 **a** Which group of people had the most say in the government of Rome?
   b In what way did the Roman senators control the life of the city?

2 **a** Which sources give us information about how Rome was governed? Explain what each source tells us.
   b At the time when the coin (Source B) was made, the senate had lost much of its power to an emperor. Can you think of any reason why the emperor was still happy to have these words stamped on coins?

3 Look carefully at Source C. Write an archaeologist's report on what you can see of this site. You will need to include:
   • a careful description of what you can see
   • a simple sketch of some of the evidence
   • a comment on how important you think this area of Rome was.

4 Why do you think the Italian government stamped 'SPQR' on something modern (Source A)?

C

The ruins of the Forum, in Rome. This was a place for debates and legal discussions.

SOURCE

2.5 Building an Empire

After the war with Carthage, Roman power spread. Rome was building an **Empire**. This is when one country conquers and controls other countries. It was not planned out beforehand. As the Romans defeated enemies, they captured many cities and people. More people were brought into the Roman army. Rome could then conquer more land. Every time the Roman army won, it got larger and became more experienced.

Victory also made some important Romans very wealthy. Commanders of armies found that war made them famous. This made them want to fight more wars. After defeating Carthage, Rome turned on Greece. Some Greeks, in Macedonia, had opposed Rome. By 148 BC, Macedonia was beaten. Soon other Greek people came under Roman control. A new province, called Asia, was set up in 133 BC. It included many Greek cities.

Roman armies were soon winning battles from southern France (Gaul) to Egypt. It seemed as if there were no limits to Roman power. Until the Roman army was defeated in Germany, in AD 9, it looked as if nothing could stop the legions.

Each new province added to the Empire was run by a **governor**, who was a member of the senate. The provinces paid taxes to the Roman authorities. With the conquest of Greece, many new ideas spread across the lands under Roman control. For the first time, many different people were being ruled by the same government. Rome was changing peoples' lives.

Countries that were not ruled by the Romans found that it was wise to keep on the right side of them. In this way, Roman power and influence spread far beyond the borders of the lands that they ruled.

A *Roman coin showing the Greek god Apollo, 10 BC.*

SOURCE

B

SOURCE

I set on the Romans, limits neither of space or time. I have given them an Empire without limits.

The Roman god Jupiter, in a play written by Virgil, in the 1st century BC.

C

SOURCE

The gods desire that the city of Rome shall be the capital of all the countries of the world. They shall practise warfare so that no humans shall be able to resist the armies of Rome.

The Roman writer Livy, writing in the 1st century BC.

D

SOURCE

Don't forget Romans, it is your special skill to rule all peoples; to impose the ways of peace. Show mercy to the defeated and crush those proud men who will not surrender!

The Roman writer Virgil, writing in the 1st century BC.

E

SOURCE

The Romans felt they had absolute moral right on their side. The Romans felt they could treat minor kingdoms in their power exactly as they wished, or exterminate whole tribes.

P. Salway, 'Roman Britain', 1981.

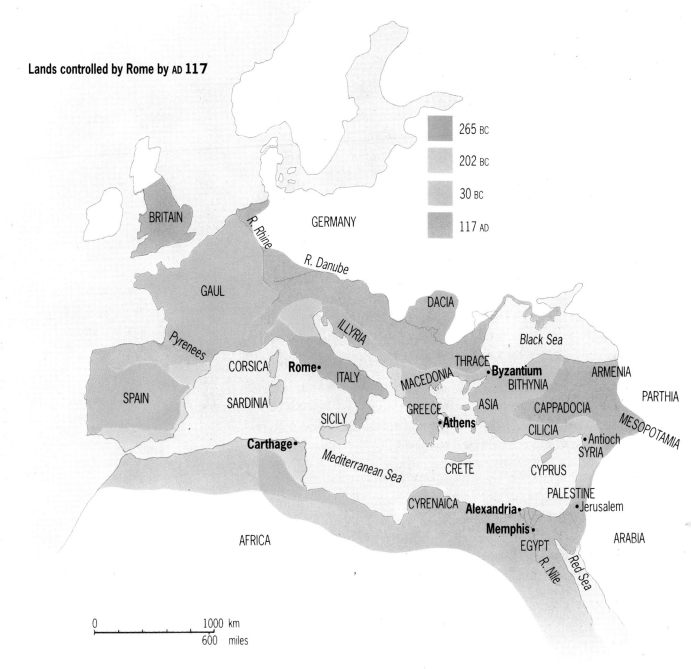

Lands controlled by Rome by AD 117

265 BC

202 BC

30 BC

117 AD

GERMANY

BRITAIN

R. Rhine

R. Danube

GAUL

DACIA

Pyrenees

ILLYRIA

Black Sea

CORSICA

Rome•

ITALY

THRACE

•Byzantium

ARMENIA

MACEDONIA

BITHYNIA

PARTHIA

SPAIN

SARDINIA

GREECE

ASIA

CAPPADOCIA

MESOPOTAMIA

SICILY

•Athens

CILICIA

•Antioch

Carthage•

SYRIA

Mediterranean Sea

CRETE

CYPRUS

PALESTINE

CYRENAICA

Alexandria•

•Jerusalem

Memphis•

ARABIA

AFRICA

EGYPT

R. Nile

Red Sea

0   1000 km

600   miles

Activities...

1 a Which, of Sources B–E, is a secondary source? How can you tell?

 b Do you think the Romans planned to build an Empire?

 c Give reasons why the Empire grew.

2 Read Source E. Now look at Sources B–D. Can you find any evidence in Sources B, C and D which agrees with the opinion of the modern historian in Source E?

3 a 'The Roman Empire was large and successful. People were glad to be members of it.' How much of this statement can be supported by looking at the map?

 b How could an historian use Source A as evidence that Greek ideas spread through the Roman Empire?

2.6 Julius Caesar

Despite the victories of Rome over its enemies, there was unrest throughout Italy during the early 1st century BC. Many Italian farmers had been ruined by the wars with Carthage. Many spent long years with the army. The rich treated the poor farmers badly. In Rome itself, the powerful citizens competed for power. The armies were loyal to their commanders, and not to the Roman senate.

Successful generals became very powerful. One, named **Sulla**, returned to Rome as a dictator. He destroyed his enemies and gave their land to his supporters. One of Sulla's supporters was **Pompey**. He defeated pirates who threatened food supplies to Rome. He had won great victories in the Middle East. Some members of the senate opposed Pompey because they were afraid of one man becoming too powerful. Pompey joined with other generals and defeated his enemies in the senate.

One of Pompey's friends was **Julius Caesar**, who became a consul in 59 BC. He led the Roman army in Gaul. Soon he had conquered Gaul. He even led two expeditions to Britain. In Rome, his enemies ordered him home. They feared that he was getting too powerful. As a governor, it was against the law for him to lead his army out of Gaul. He broke this law. He crossed the river Rubicon (the boundary of his province) in 49 BC, and invaded Italy. He faced enemies in Italy, and in the Roman provinces of Spain, Egypt and Africa. His old friend Pompey now tried to control him. Caesar fought back. He chased Pompey to Egypt, where Pompey was murdered. While he was there, Caesar became involved in a civil war that was taking place between the Egyptians. For a short while he was the lover of Cleopatra, the Egyptian Queen. By 45 BC, Caesar had defeated most of his enemies.

Julius Caesar put his friends in places of power in the senate. They elected him dictator for life. He ruled Rome as if he were a king. Many powerful senators were frightened of him. They felt he had too much power, so on 15 March 44 BC, a group of them murdered him.

A SOURCE

There is a story of him [Caesar] joking and playing at dice with some pirates who captured him. One of his jokes was that he would crucify them when he was freed. The pirates laughed, but crucify them he did.

J. M. Roberts, 'History of the World', 1980.

B SOURCE

Caesar would have sought glory and booty [loot] whatever the situation, as part of the normal career of an ambitious nobleman.

B. Dobson, 'Hadrian's Wall', 1976.

C SOURCE

Caesar marched quickly to Spain to defeat seven legions. They were then mildly treated in order to win over as many as possible of the soldiers.

J. M. Roberts, 'History of the World', 1980.

D SOURCE

There is much debate on whether he had a long term plan in life, always intent on supreme power, or was an opportunist. [A person who makes the most of any situation which will help them but does not plan it out in advance.]

P. Salway, 'Roman Britain', 1981.

Some of Julius Caesar's actions.

Gave land to poor citizens.

Reformed the laws.

Ruled like a king.

Built many fine buildings.

Put his friends in powerful positions.

Named a month after himself (July).

Wore purple robes, like a king.

Introduced a new calendar.

Helped many people in Spain and Gaul to become citizens.

Put up his own statue among the statues of the old kings of Rome.

E

SOURCE

A bust [head and shoulders] of Julius Caesar.

Activities...

1 a Look at the list of Julius Caesar's actions. These actions would have had different **consequences**. Some actions would have been popular. Some would have been unpopular. Decide which actions from the list should go under each of these headings.
Popular actions
Unpopular actions

b Are there any actions which would have been popular with some people but unpopular with others? Which ones are they?

2 a Sources A and C give very different impressions of Caesar. Why do you think he might have acted so differently in these two situations?

b According to the writer of Source D, what is it about Caesar that historians cannot agree on?

c Look at Source B. Which side of the argument mentioned in Source D does this writer seem to support?

3 Which of the sources in this Unit would be least helpful in making a study of the life of Julius Caesar? Explain your answer.

2.7 Case Study 1: Caesar Invades Britain

In 55 and 54 BC, Julius Caesar led an army to Britain. No Roman general had ever done this before, but this did not mean that the Romans knew nothing about Britain. For many years both Greek and Roman traders had travelled to Britain to buy and sell goods. Also, the Romans had conquered large areas of Gaul (now France) and turned it into a province. In Gaul, the Romans heard many stories about the island of Britain. The Romans also knew that some of their enemies in Gaul were being helped by people from Britain.

When Caesar led his expedition in 55 BC, he came to discover more about Britain and its people. He also came to frighten those British leaders who were helping his enemies in Gaul. A victory would also have made him more famous. Caesar did not bring a large army with him. Bad weather meant that even some of these soldiers were unable to cross the sea.

When Caesar reached Britain he found that the British were armed and ready for him. At first, his soldiers were too frightened to leave their boats. It was only when the standard bearer of the Tenth Legion leapt into the water that the others followed.

Eventually, Caesar's soldiers fought their way ashore. However, four days after he landed, a storm wrecked many of Caesar's ships. He was forced to repair them and take his men back to Gaul.

In 54 BC he came back with a larger army. Marching inland, through modern Kent, he fought a number of battles against the British. Next, he crossed the river Thames. Some of the British went over to the Roman side. In the end, Cassivellaunus, the leader of the British, asked for peace. Caesar took some British hostages, to make sure that their families were friendly towards Rome. He also demanded that the British should pay a sum of money to the Romans every year. Then Caesar returned to Gaul. Britain did not actually become a Roman province until it was invaded again in AD 43.

Two thousand years ago Roman writers disagreed about how worthwhile the invasion of Britain was. In this Unit you will examine some of these primary sources. It is important to remember that one of the reasons why modern historians disagree about what happened in history is because primary sources do not always agree. Each of the sources in the Unit describes Britain.

A **SOURCE**

There is an infinite number of men, very many buildings and very large herds. They use either bronze or gold money. There is timber of every kind.

Julius Caesar writing about Britain. He lived from 100–44 BC.

B **SOURCE**

Their way of life is modest and they are free from the luxuries which come from being rich. The island is thickly populated, much tin is also carried from the British Isles to Gaul.

Diodorus Siculus, writing in about 30 BC.

C **SOURCE**

Britain has gold and silver and other metals. The ocean, too, produces pearls.

The Roman writer Tacitus who lived from AD 56–115.

D

SOURCE

Twice he [Caesar] crossed the narrow sea and, fighting many battles there, he hurt the enemy more than gained riches for his own men. It was not possible to take anything from people who were poor.

The Roman writer Plutarch who lived from AD 50–125.

E

SOURCE

He [Caesar] also invaded Britain and defeated the natives from whom he took a large amount of money as well as hostages. Fresh water pearls seem to have been the attraction which led to his invasion.

Suetonius, writing in about AD 120.

F

SOURCE

The inhabitants of this island refuse money and get what they need by swapping things rather than by buying.

Solinus, writing in about AD 200.

G

SOURCE

Some suppose that the Britons are named this because they are 'brutes'. They are a people living in the ocean, cut off by the sea. It is as if they were outside the world.

Isidorus Hispalensis, writing in about AD 620.

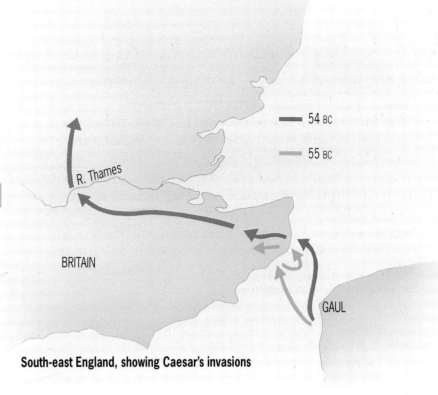

South-east England, showing Caesar's invasions

Activities...

1 a Why do historians disagree with each other about why Caesar came to Britain?

b Look at Sources A–G in this Unit. Make a list of anything mentioned in them which might have made Britain seem attractive to Caesar.

c Now put your list in order of importance. Put the most important at number 1, the next most important at number 2, and so on. Explain your first choice.

2 a Each of Sources A–G describes Britain. What else would you need to know about the writers of these sources, in order to decide if they can be trusted?

b Sometimes a source is **biased**. This means that it only tells one side of a story. It can give too good, or too bad, an account. Which source gives the most biased account **against** the British?
Explain why you made this choice.

3 a Look at Source A. Why did Caesar think Britain was attractive?

b Now look at the other sources. Which sources agree with Source A?

c Which sources disagree with Source A?

d Which sources give you information, not mentioned by Caesar? (You may find that some sources appear in more than one answer.)

2.8 Case Study 2: Claudius Invades Britain

Julius Caesar visited Britain twice. He fought battles but did not make Britain a province of the Roman Empire. A later emperor, Caligula, planned to make Britain a province of the Empire. He even went as far as bringing a great army to Gaul for the invasion but, at the last minute, he called it off.

In AD 43, **Emperor Claudius** ordered an invasion of Britain. He had been made emperor when Caligula was murdered. Claudius wanted people to think he was a good general. He invaded Britain to prove this. His excuse for the invasion was that a British king friendly to Rome, Verica, had been driven out of his lands by his enemies.

The Roman army landed near Richborough, in what is now Kent. It was led by **Aulus Plautius**. In a great battle, fought at the River Medway, the British were thrown back. When Aulus Plautius reached the Thames, he stopped his advance while he waited for Claudius to arrive from Rome. Claudius was in Britain for sixteen days. During this time, he defeated the British who opposed him in south-east Britain. Their capital, at Colchester, was captured.

Claudius went back to Rome, but the army continued with the conquest of Britain. The Ninth and Fourteenth Legions advanced north and west from Colchester. The Second Legion continued a march along the south coast. Its general, **Vespasian**, captured over twenty British forts, in Hampshire, Dorset and Somerset.

In this Unit you will read different primary sources giving accounts of the invasion. Once again, they do not all tell the same story. You will also read different secondary sources. This will show you how historians use different primary sources and come to different conclusions.

A SOURCE

In AD 43 the Emperor Claudius finally invaded our island with four legions of Roman soldiers. They landed in Kent and marched inland. Some Britons welcomed them, some fought hard against them, but bit by bit they conquered the whole of what we now call England and Wales.

J. Liversidge, 'Roman Britain', 1958.

B SOURCE

The Britons made a valiant effort to defend the line of the river Medway and were only driven off after a fierce two-day battle. Claudius then put in an appearance to claim the victory his subordinate [junior] had already won.

R. Selman, 'Roman Britain', 1956.

C SOURCE

He had received the surrender of eleven British kings, defeated without casualties, and brought barbarian peoples beyond the ocean for the first time under Roman rule.

Inscription in Rome, from the 1st century AD.

D SOURCE

Claudius took the triumph without any effort of his own.

The Jewish historian Josephus, writing in the 1st century AD.

E

SOURCE

Having crossed to Britain, Claudius joined the forces which were waiting for him at the Thames. Taking over command, he crossed it and, coming to grips with the forces assembled to oppose him, he defeated them and captured Colchester.

Cassius Dio, who lived from AD 160–230.

F

SOURCE

Vespasian fought thirty times with the enemy. He defeated two powerful tribes and captured the Isle of Wight, under the leadership, partly of Aulus Plautius, partly of Claudius himself. Claudius fought no battles and suffered no casualties.

Suetonius Tranquillus, writing in about AD 120.

Maiden Castle, in Dorset. A hill fort attacked by Roman soldiers.

Activities...

1 a Which of the sources are primary sources? How can you tell?

b According to Source B, what events had taken place before the arrival of Emperor Claudius?

c According to Source B, would it have mattered if Claudius had not come to Britain? Explain your answer.

2 a The writer Josephus was a friend of the Roman general Vespasian (mentioned in Source F). Do you think his version of the invasion can be trusted? Explain your answer.

b Source C is an account of the invasion by the Roman government of Claudius. Do you think this version of the invasion can be trusted? Explain your answer.

c Read Sources A and B. Which of the primary sources in this Unit do you think each writer has used?

3 In what ways do the primary sources disagree about the part played by Claudius in the invasion of Britain?

2.9 The Emperors

When Julius Caesar was murdered, in 44 BC, his great nephew **Octavian** came to Rome to take revenge. He had been made Caesar's heir and adopted son. Octavian worked with one of Caesar's supporters – **Mark Anthony** – to destroy Caesar's murderers.

Octavian and Mark Anthony soon quarrelled. At the **Battle of Actium** (31 BC), Mark Anthony was defeated. He and his lover, Cleopatra of Egypt, committed suicide.

Octavian was left in control. Rome had been weakened by twenty years of civil war. He set out to make Rome strong again. He also set about transforming its laws.

In 27 BC, he took the title of **Augustus**. It means 'majestic', or 'noble'. He was now the complete ruler of Rome, although he was careful to show respect to the old Republic. He was also Chief Priest of Rome. Most historians use this date to divide up Roman history. The years before 27 BC they call **The Republic**. The years after they call **The Empire**. From this time onwards, Rome was ruled by emperors. Actually, as we have seen, Rome was building an empire long before 27 BC. Also, Julius Caesar had held as much power as some of the later emperors. However, historians use this date because Augustus set himself up as a more powerful ruler than any other that Rome had known.

When Augustus died in AD 14, power passed to his stepson, Tiberius. Rome was now ruled by a royal family.

B SOURCE

A Roman silver coin made in 28 BC. It celebrates the addition of Egypt to the Empire, by Augustus.

A SOURCE

A Roman gold coin made in 20 BC. It celebrates the addition of Armenia to the Empire, by Augustus.

C SOURCE

Their loyalty was to the family of the emperor, not to the Senate and people.

P. Salway describing the Roman army during the Empire. 'Roman Britain', 1981.

A portrait of the head of Augustus, made of glass. It was probably made soon after his death, in AD 14. However, it makes him appear as if he were a young man.

The army, though, influenced who would be emperor. Tiberius was followed by Caligula, Claudius and Nero. All three were murdered. When Nero was murdered in AD 68, a civil war followed. In AD 69, there were four rival emperors. The war was eventually won in the same year by Vespasian, the general who had fought in Britain.

In AD 192, there was civil war again which lasted until AD 197. Different armies backed different rival emperors. The Empire suffered greatly in these civil wars, as rival generals and nobles fought to become emperor. The emperors became afraid of letting their generals become too powerful and successful. Such a general might try to become emperor himself. As a result, the Empire stopped growing.

Worse than this, the enemies of Rome took advantage of those times when Rome was weakened by civil war.

E

SOURCE

At home, Augustus improved the state of the country and its people. Abroad, his armies fought battles to win peace through victory. Kings beyond the frontier of the Empire made pacts with him. Ambassadors and princes came from far away with valuable presents: from Persia and India, from Britain and Romania. The senate and people of Rome honoured him for his 'courage, mercy, justice and piety'. His enemies in Rome did not live to tell a different story.

A. Millard, 'Discoveries from the Time of Jesus', 1990.

Activities...

1 a Give one reason why having emperors may be said to have weakened Rome.

b Give one reason for, and one reason against, treating the year 27 BC as vitally important in the history of Rome.

c What important change of attitude is mentioned in Source C? Why was this change important?

2 a Look at Sources A and B. How did Augustus spread the news about his victories?

b Do you think this affects the way historians think about him?

3 Why did the person who made Source D make Augustus look like a younger man?

4 a Source E tells us many good things about Augustus. Why does the writer think that people only ever heard good things said about him?

b Does this affect the way historians should look at sources of evidence from the time of the Roman emperors?

3.1 Citizens

A **citizen** is a member of a country. As a citizen, a person has certain **rights** and **duties.** A person's rights are those things that they are allowed to do by law. A person's duties are those things that they have to do. Roman citizens had special rights. They could serve in the army, and were protected by the law. They could vote in government elections. They were protected from harsh treatment and certain punishments. They also had duties, such as paying full Roman taxes.

As Roman power spread, the people in some conquered cities were allowed to become citizens. In 91 BC, there was a revolt in Italy. It was led by people who demanded the rights of Roman citizens. It was seen as a good thing to be a citizen.

When the army conquered foreign lands, Roman citizens soon followed. They came as tax collectors, traders and land owners. Ex-soldiers were given land in captured provinces. Cities made up of these citizens were called **colonia**. They often made money out of the natives. Augustus started 75 colonia in foreign lands. They spread the Roman way of life and helped to control and run the Empire. It was also a way to get troublesome people away from Rome! When the leaders of conquered people accepted Roman rule, they were allowed to become citizens. This encouraged them to live and act like Romans.

In AD 212, all free members of the Empire were made citizens. This meant that everyone could be fully taxed.

B **SOURCE**

Gaul is packed with traders, crammed with citizens. No Gaul does business without involving a Roman citizen. Not a penny changes hands without the deal being recorded by a Roman citizen.

The Roman writer Cicero, writing in 74 BC.

C **SOURCE**

What use are laws when money calls all the tunes and people without a gentleman's income have no real rights at all?

The Roman writer Petronius, writing in the 1st century AD. He is talking about poor citizens.

A **SOURCE**

Then the officials tore the clothes off Paul and Silas and ordered them to be whipped. After a severe beating they were thrown into jail. The next morning the Roman authorities sent officers with the order, 'Let these men go'. But Paul said to the officers, 'We were not found guilty of any crime, yet they whipped us in public – and we are Roman citizens. Then they threw us in prison.' The officers reported these words to the Roman officials, and when they heard that Paul and Silas were Roman citizens, they were afraid.

The experiences of two early Christians in the Roman colonia of Philippi (in modern Greece), in about AD 50. It is recorded in the Acts of the Apostles, chapter 16.

Some of the people who were not citizens were **slaves**. A slave is someone who is not free. A slave belongs to a person in the way that a horse, or a piece of furniture does. A slave could be bought and sold and had no rights. However, they were protected from the worst treatment by laws passed by the Emperors Augustus and Hadrian. Most slaves were either the children of slaves, or had been captured in wars with the Roman army.

Some of them were made to do hard work, although others were educated. These educated slaves were used as teachers, and some became quite powerful servants of the emperors. Sometimes these important slaves were able to buy their own freedom. Usually, though, slaves only became free if they were freed by their masters or mistresses. They were then called **freedmen**. These freedmen often did important jobs for the emperor. Some even became wealthy, often as merchants, buying and selling goods.

Tombstone of a woman named Regina who was a British slave. She was bought by a soldier who freed her and married her.

Activities...

1 **a** Why was it regarded as a 'good' thing to be a Roman citizen?
   b What did the Emperors Augustus and Hadrian do to help slaves?

2 Look at Source B, which is about actions of Roman citizens in Gaul. If you were one of the non-citizens living in Gaul, how would you feel about what these citizens were doing in your country?

3 **a** In Source A, why were the Roman officials afraid?
   b Which of the sources could be used as evidence that a person's position in Roman society was often decided by someone else?
   c 'If a person became a Roman citizen, life was made easy for them.' Using all of the sources, say whether you agree or disagree with this statement. Explain your answer.

3.2 Barbarians

People who lived outside the Empire were known as **barbarians**. This is a Greek word, used to show that they did not speak a respected language. Respected languages were Greek, and then Latin. These were the main languages of the Empire.

Barbarians did not live, dress, or speak like Roman citizens. Romans often thought of them as uncivilized savages. In reality, they had their own ways of life. The barbarians were very attracted to the wealth of the Empire, and often hoped to share in it. Some, especially towards the end of the Roman Empire, served as soldiers in the Roman army. Others raided the lands of the Empire, to steal. Some barbarians tried to settle inside the Empire and live like Romans. As Rome grew weak, the powerful barbarian peoples became a threat to the Empire.

The Romans had mixed views of the barbarians. Often they looked down on them. At other times they were willing to use them if they could. Some Romans even found it fashionable to copy attractive characteristics of barbarian people. The sources in this Unit will show you some of these mixed views.

A SOURCE

Too tall. Lank blond, or red hair. Light blue eyes. Upturned noses. Huge bellies. Simple minds. Quick tempers. Brave. Reckless. Drunken. Lazy. Gambling and boastful.

A modern historian's list of Roman descriptions of northern barbarians. From L. A. Thompson, 'Romans and Blacks', 1989.

B SOURCE

Pale brown faces. Straight nose. Bright brown eyes. Brown hair. Thin lips. Not too tall.

A modern historian's list of Roman descriptions of perfect appearance. From L. A. Thompson, 'Romans and Blacks', 1989.

C SOURCE

We change our hair colour to blond, because men find us more attractive that way.

The Roman poet Martial on how Roman women copied barbarian looks. Written in the 1st century AD.

D SOURCE

Africans have whiter souls than the whitest of Greeks.

Roman comment, from about AD 250.

E

SOURCE

The kingdom of Ethiopia is a fertile and rich wonderland, possessing an abundance of gold and a royal family descended from the gods.

From a Roman geography book written in about AD *250.*

F

SOURCE

In 151 BC Sulpicius Galga, who had massacred thousands of Lusitanians [from modern Portugal] after they had surrendered to him, was acquitted [found not guilty] at his trial. Very few people in Rome cared much about what happened to the Barbarians.

T. Cornell and J. Matthews, 'Atlas of the Roman World', 1982.

G

Roman gold and silver coins, found in the village of Ginderup, in Denmark. These coins were probably buried in about AD *100.*

The people who lived in Ginderup were not members of the Roman Empire. They lived far beyond its frontiers. Archaeologists believe that the coins probably belonged to a barbarian tribesman who served in the Roman army. He may have buried the coins, for safety, when he returned to his native village.

SOURCE

Activities...

1 a What kinds of people did the Romans call barbarians?
  b Give two ways in which barbarians shared in the wealth of Rome.

2 a Over time, some Roman writers changed their minds about some of the barbarians. They wrote about barbarian lands as if they were 'fairy-tale' places. Which of the sources shows this view of the barbarians?
  b Is there anything about Source E which might make you distrust it as an accurate source of information?

3 a Read Sources A and B. Now make up two police identikit pictures, one for each of these Roman views of what barbarians and Romans looked like.
  b Which source shows that not all Romans thought barbarians were unattractive?
  c How important is this source, in your opinion?

4 a What does Source G tell us about the relationship between Romans and barbarians?
  b What did the writer of Source D mean? How could an historian use this source to show that not all Romans looked down on barbarians?

3.3 The Family

The family was very important to the Romans. Each family was under the control of the father. In Latin, he was called the **paterfamilias** (the father of the family). He had complete control over all relatives and servants in the house. His sons stayed under his control until he died.

The paterfamilias led the family in its worship of the gods. It was believed that household gods looked after each family.

Related families were grouped together and shared a name. A group of related families was known as a **gens**. Each member of the gens had his or her personal name and the name of the gens. This showed which group of families they belonged to.

Women were under the control of their husbands or fathers. However, they controlled how the house was run. The Roman mother was called the **materfamilias** (mother of the family).

Some women tried to be more independent and educated. Roman writers were not always happy with this. They felt a woman's place was running the home.

This is how families were organized in Rome. However, we must remember that the Roman Empire was very large. There were some groups of people living within the Empire who organized themselves differently. For example, in Britain during the 1st century AD there were women who were very powerful rulers. One, named Boudicca, ruled a tribe called the Iceni. Another, named Cartimandua, ruled a tribe called the Brigantes.

B SOURCE

All men rule over women. We Romans rule over all men and our wives rule over us!

The Roman writer Cato, who lived from 234–149 BC.

A SOURCE

Statues of a family from Palmira, in modern Syria. They are members of the Roman Empire but are dressed in middle-eastern clothes from the 2nd century AD. These people would have spoken the Palmirene language instead of Latin. They would have followed Arab ways of life, not Roman ones.

Bathing a baby. A carving from Rome.

Activities...

1 The beginnings and ends of the following sentences have been mixed up. Match the correct head to its tail. In each case the tail happened because the head took place. This makes the head a **cause** and the tail a **consequence**.

Heads	**Tails**
Families were grouped together	so some writers condemned them.
Fathers controlled the family	and each person had a gens name.
Some women tried to act freely	with different family types.
The Empire was very large	so wives were not free to act.

2 Explain why it would be very difficult for an historian to say that family life and the relationship between men and women was the same for all people across the Empire.

3 a How does Source C illustrate the Roman view of a woman's place in life?

b Compare Sources B and D. How do these two writers differ in their description of the way women acted within marriage and the family?

You were a faithful wife to me, and an obedient one. You were kind, gracious and friendly. You worked hard at your spinning. You did not dress so as to be noticed, nor did you show off your running of the house. You did your duty to the household. You tended my mother as if she had been your own.

A Roman description of a faithful wife from the 1st century BC.

3.4 Transport

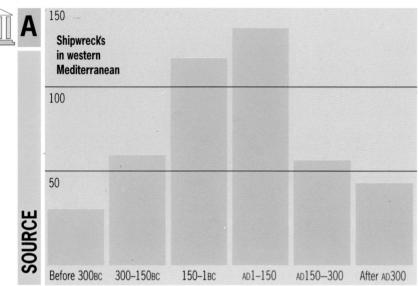

A

SOURCE

Shipwrecks in western Mediterranean

150	
100	
50	

Before 300BC   300–150BC   150–1BC   AD1–150   AD150–300   After AD300

This graph shows the number of ancient ships found by underwater archaeologists, in the western Mediterranean.

C

SOURCE

The roads were carried straight across the countryside, were paved with cut stones and supported underneath with masses of tightly-packed gravel. Hollows were filled in and ravines that cut across the route were bridged.

Plutarch, who lived from AD 50–120, describing roads built by the army.

The Roman Empire needed good transport routes. The army had to move about quickly. Food had to be carried to Rome. Taxes had to be collected. The evidence which has survived about Roman transport shows us just how important it was. There were four main forms of transport: by road; by sea; by river; by canal. Many clues remain about each sort.

▼ *Painting of a Roman ship from Ostia, near Rome. The ship was called the 'Isis Giminiana'. The captain's name was Farnaces.*

B

SOURCE

D

SOURCE

I think I should bring to your attention any plan which is worthy of your immortal name and glory. There is a large lake, near Nicomedia, across which marble, food, and timber for building are easily brought by boat as far as the main road.

After this everything has to be taken to the sea by cart, with great difficulty and increased cost. To connect the lake with the sea would require a lot of workmen but there are plenty of them available.

◀ *Letter from Pliny, Governor of Bythinia, in modern Turkey, to the Emperor Trajan, in about AD 112. He is writing about a plan for a new canal.*

Thousands of miles of Roman roads survive to be studied. They were so well made, that archaeologists can tell that a lot of effort went into building them. We also know about the roads from other sources of evidence. Some of these sources are descriptions of how the roads were made. Some are descriptions of the best way to get from one place to another, and the distance between the places. These sources are called **itineraries**. Several have survived from Roman times. One, called the **Peutinger Table**, is a map of the world known to the Romans. It shows towns and roads. Another, called the **Antonine Itinerary**, lists 225 routes around the Empire and the distance between places.

Other forms of evidence, like the **Acts of the Apostles** in the New Testament, show us that people were able to travel around fairly easily. We also know that the Romans travelled by sea. There are mosaics and paintings of ships. These show us what Roman boats looked like. Official documents have survived. These tell us that thousands of tons of grain were carried, by ship, from north Africa to Rome. Underwater archaeologists have even found the remains of Roman ships. Some of these sank at sea. Others sank in rivers and harbours. Roman ships have been found in the river Thames, near the Roman port of Londinium (London). One, found at Madrague de Giens, off the south coast of France, was carrying wine and fine pottery.

The Romans also dug man-made rivers. These are called **canals**. The rivers Rhine and Meuse (in Germany) were linked by a canal. Another canal called the Car Dyke carried goods in eastern England. As well as these surviving canals, we also have evidence in Roman documents, explaining why canals were useful. All of these surviving primary sources give us information about the importance of travel in the Empire.

Activities...

1 a Why did the Roman Empire need good forms of transport?

b Look at Source D. Why did Pliny think that building a canal would be a good idea?

c How did he make it more likely that Trajan would agree with his plan?

2 a How could an historian use the work of underwater archaeologists to support the idea that travel by sea increased when the Roman Empire was at its most powerful (between 150 BC and AD 300)?

b Can you think of any reasons why the graph (Source A) might not tell us everything we need to know about the number of ships that were wrecked during the Roman Empire?

3 a Using Sources B and C, explain what they tell historians about Roman transport.

b Which source do you think is the most useful? Explain your answer.

3.5 Trade in the Empire

 The Roman Empire was very good for trade, for a number of reasons. The large Roman army needed to be supplied with food, clothes, pottery and weapons. Soldiers and other people who worked for the government were paid with coins. They wanted to buy things with their money.

The Romans brought peace to many countries. This was called the **Pax Romana**. It made it safe to travel long distances. Good roads helped as well. Roman towns were useful places in which people could meet to buy and sell goods.

Most trade began with supplying the army with what it needed. Roman merchants organized this. They also helped the government to buy grain to feed the people living in Rome. These merchants were called **negotiatores**. They bought things like wine, food and pottery and transported them to the army.

The negotiatores began to see that they could sell things to ordinary people, too. Soon they were carrying these things on the ships loaded with army supplies. Expensive pottery and glass could be carried on ships loaded with olive oil, wine or grain. The pottery or glass took up only a little space. However, it could be sold for high prices. Pottery from Italy and Africa was carried as far as Germany, Britain and the province of Gaul.

A carving of a Roman ship carrying wine barrels.

A

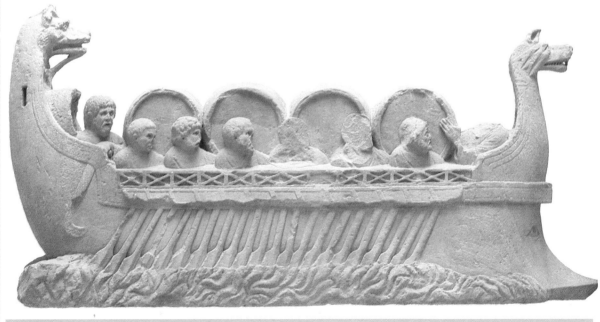

SOURCE

B

SOURCE

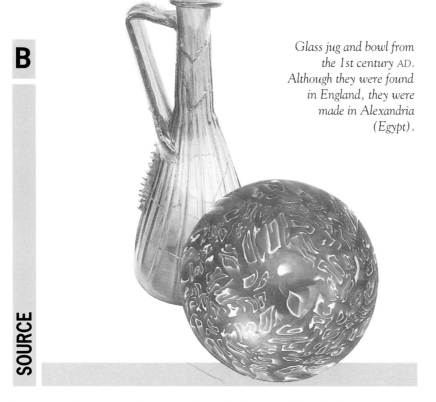

Glass jug and bowl from the 1st century AD. Although they were found in England, they were made in Alexandria (Egypt).

Many craftsmen and women found they could sell their goods to more people than ever before. In the town of Lyons (in Roman Gaul), negotiatores put together loads of goods to be taken as far away as Britain and the rivers Rhine and Danube.

Not all the trade was carried out by rich negotiatores. All over the Empire, farmers, potters and metal workers saw a chance to make more money. They sold their goods at local towns and markets.

C

SOURCE

Sunken grain storage jars. From Ostia, the port of Rome.

Activities...

1 **a** Find four ways in which the Roman Empire helped to make trade easier.
   b Explain how each of these ways would have encouraged buying and selling.

2 Look at Source A. Imagine that you are making a study of trade within the Roman Empire. What other information would you like to have about this ship, in order to use it as evidence?

3 Look carefully at Source B.
   a What problems would a Roman merchant face, when sending these a long distance?
   b Suggest reasons why this glass jug and bowl would have been expensive.

4 'The city of Rome lived off large amounts of grain, brought from north Africa.' Is there any information in the sources to support this statement?

3.6 Roman Towns and Cities

The Romans are famous for their **towns** and **cities**. The Romans did not invent them. People around the Mediterranean had lived in towns for many centuries. What the Romans did was make them bigger than ever before, and build them in places which had never had towns before. The people who lived in the biggest Roman towns were given the right to run them. We call these very large towns, cities. Even after hundreds of years the ruins of cities survive, when other kinds of evidence decays. This helps to explain why people think of towns when they think of the Romans.

The larger Roman towns were usually carefully planned. They had a meeting place called the **forum**. Government officials often had their own building, called the **basilica**. From here they could control the running of the town and the land around it. Some large towns, like Calleva (Silchester), in England, were originally less carefully planned. But as people became more like their new Roman rulers they copied the Roman ways of planning towns. Smaller towns were never well planned. They had few big buildings.

▶ *The walls of many towns were improved in the 4th century AD. New towers were added, which stood out from the walls. They made it harder for enemies to attack the town. The ditches around the towns were also redug.*

A *The walls and towers of the Roman city of Constantinople, in modern Turkey. Walls were built around towns and cities to keep them safe from attack. These walls and towers were built in about AD 413.*

SOURCE

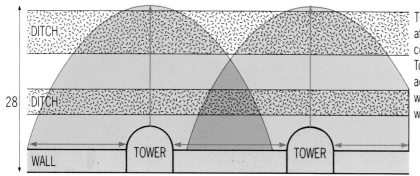

Town defences after the 4th century AD. Towers were added to the walls. Ditches were redug.

Area reached by weapons fired from the walls.

Area in front of walls, out of reach of defenders weapons.

Direction and distance weapons could be fired from town walls.

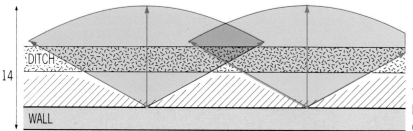

Town defences before the 4th century AD.

The Roman government controlled the new provinces through towns and cities. People came to towns to pay taxes. In order to pay their taxes, they sold what they had grown, or made, for Roman coins. Any money left after they had paid their taxes could be spent in the towns. This encouraged other people to bring their goods to town, to sell for cash. Roman taxes gave life to the towns. When the taxes stopped, people stopped buying and selling and the towns came to an end.

SOURCE

B

A gold coin. This one shows the Emperor Antonius Pius, who was emperor between AD 138 and 161. It would have been worth more than a small farmer earned in one year. Taxes had to be paid in gold and silver coins.

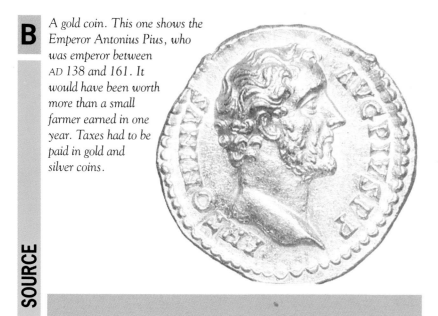

Activities...

1 Explain how Roman taxes helped to encourage the growth of towns.

2 In what ways could historians use the remains of Roman towns to show how well organized the Romans were?

3 a Archaeologists find lots of copper coins on Roman sites. They very rarely find gold ones. Explain why this is so.
  b Look at the diagram showing the changes in town walls. Why would the new defences have made it harder to attack a town?
  c How might an historian tell that the walls of Constantinople (Source A) were built after the 4th century AD?

3.7 Buildings in Towns and Cities

Carving showing a Roman shop.

The remains of Roman towns show some of the skills used by Roman planners and builders. A person who plans how a building should be built is called an **architect**. Roman architects planned fine buildings with great **arches** and **domes**. Roman builders invented **concrete**. This is a mixture of water, sand, stone and cement. Concrete helped to make the buildings strong.

Government buildings were made out of fine stone and paid for with money raised in taxes. Marble is a beautiful stone and the government controlled its supply. This was a way of making money, and making sure there was enough marble for government buildings.

B

SOURCE

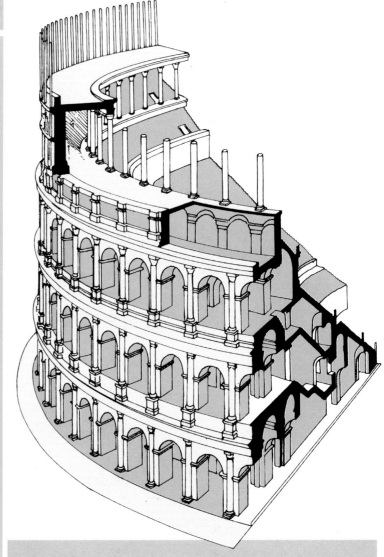

A modern drawing which shows Roman building skills. The weight of the whole building is carried by the arches. This downward force is spread sideways by the arches. A complete circle of arches stops this sideways force from breaking the arches apart.

SOURCE

◄ *The Roman baths at the city of Aqua Sulis (Bath) England. Everything above the square bases of the pillars is a Victorian reconstruction of what the baths might have looked like. It is not Roman, it was made in the 19th century* AD.

Most buildings were made from whatever local stone was available. Others were made from wood and tiles. In the Middle East mud bricks were used for building.

As well as fine buildings, towns contained lots of shops. In this Unit you will find examples of the kinds of building skills and shops found in Roman towns.

D

SOURCE

◄ *Carving showing a Roman shop.*

Activities...

1 How did the skills of Roman architects and builders help to make Roman buildings so strong?

2 Why should an historian be very careful about using Source C as evidence for how the Romans built the baths at Bath?

3 **a** Look carefully at Sources A and D. Write a report of what you can see in these sources.
   b What kinds of shops do you think that these were?

4 What other questions would you like to ask about Sources A and D?

5 Imagine that you have been taken to the remains of a Roman town. You have not been told where you are. Give one way in which you might be able to tell which part of the Empire the town was in.

3.8 Living in Towns and Cities

◀ *Public toilets in the Roman town of Thugga (Tunisia) in north Africa.*

By AD 1, over one million people lived in Rome. The majority lived in blocks of flats, called **insulae**. The poorer Romans rented these flats.

The flats were badly built. They had no heating or running water. People could be turned out of their rooms by their landlords. Buildings often collapsed, or caught fire.

There were sewers under the streets, but only the houses of the rich were able to use them. Poorer people were tempted to dump their rubbish in the street, or in the river Tiber. Streets were filthy, dark and dangerous, and disease was common.

▼ *A Roman aqueduct, in Tunisia. An aqueduct carries water from one place to another. This aqueduct carried water 60 miles to the Roman city of Carthage. It was built between AD 117 and 138.*

B

SOURCE

C

Gladiators fighting animals and a prisoner being fed to a leopard. This mosaic is from Zliten, in modern Libya, north Africa.

Many poorer citizens were unhappy with their lives. So powerful leaders would put on great entertainments to try to keep them happy, or to win their support. Wealthy people might pay for a chariot team. Fierce support for a team could lead to riots. Another popular entertainment was watching men and women fight to the death. These people were known as **gladiators**. Also, many people went to the theatre to watch plays being performed.

Activities...

1 **a** Why did wealthy Romans spend so much money putting on entertainments for poorer citizens?
   b Why was Rome such an unhealthy city?

2 Which sources provide you with evidence about health and hygiene in Roman towns? What impression do those sources give you about this subject?

3 **a** Why was the aquaduct in Source B covered?
   b What information does Source D give you about the importance of theatres in Roman towns?
   c Imagine that you are a citizen, watching the scene in Source C. Describe the entertainment put on for your enjoyment.

D

Theatre in the city of Ephesus, in modern Turkey. It was built between 250 and 150 BC. It was altered in the 1st century AD.

3.9 Life in the Countryside

Most people living in the Roman Empire did not live in large cities and towns. They lived in the countryside where there were smaller towns, villages, groups of farms and single farms. Most people in the Empire worked on the land.

Most rich Romans owned large areas of land, called **estates**. Estates were scattered all over the Empire. In the 4th century AD, a wealthy woman named Melania owned land in Italy, Sicily, Africa, Spain and Britain. Many of the people farming the land would have been tenants of a rich landowner like Melania. These tenants did not own the land, they rented it. Some poorer farmers worked on the landowner's land without pay, as a form of rent.

The Empire covered areas with very different climates and different types of farming. In all areas, most of the land was divided into estates. From as far apart as Gaul (modern France) and modern Bulgaria there is evidence that villages of tenants lay nearby the great houses of the landowners. Sometimes the landowner employed a manager who lived in the great house and ran the estate.

B **SOURCE**

Although they were altered over the years, their basic plan did not change. A door led from the street into a paved courtyard and various rooms opened from that. Stone pillars helped to hold up the flat roof and there were stone steps to climb up on to the roof.

A modern archaeologist's description of village houses in the Middle East during the Roman Empire.

A **SOURCE**

A modern reconstruction of a dining room in a Roman country house, in about AD 350.

Many of the farms and villages changed little during the time they were ruled by Rome. Here and there, though, a better off farmer might copy Roman fashions. These 'Roman farms' often had tiled roofs, painted plaster walls, mosaic floors and central heating. Other farmers bought pottery, tools and brooches. When archaeologists find lots of Roman pottery on the site of a farm, they know that the people who lived there were making the most of Roman trade. They were growing more crops and looking after more animals than they needed in order to feed themselves. They sold any extra, or **surplus**, food and animals in order to get money to pay their taxes. But they also managed to buy things for themselves – most people could afford at least to buy some Roman-style pottery.

C **SOURCE**

Roman mosaic from Tunisia. It shows a thatched house from Roman north Africa.

D **SOURCE**

Activities...

1 **a** Describe the appearance of the farmhouses shown in Sources C and D.
   b What do you think they are made from?
   c Many of these farmhouses would not have survived for archaeologists to discover. Why is this?

2 **a** Read Source B. Draw a plan of this kind of country house.
   b How would this house have been different from the ones shown in Sources C and D?

3 Look at Source A. Do you think that a room like this would have been found in farmhouses like Sources C and D? Explain your answer.

4 If you were an archaeologist, what evidence would you use to tell whether a farmer had followed Roman fashions?

5 'The countryside was the same throughout the Roman Empire.' Using the sources as evidence, say whether you agree or disagree with this statement, and why.

◀ *A modern reconstruction of a farmhouse from Hampshire in England. Many poorer farmers would have lived in houses like this, in Roman Britain.*

3.10 Roman Villas

Villa is a Latin word which means both 'house in the countryside' and 'farm'. Historians and archaeologists disagree about exactly which buildings should be called villas. Some think that farms in towns should be called villas, but most insist that a villa must be in the countryside. Some say that any grand house in the countryside should be called a villa, but most think that a villa should be at the centre of a farm or large estate. All agree that villas must be **romanized** buildings, not farms built in the native style.

Some villas were huge luxury houses. They had wide corridors, rectangular rooms, bath houses and underfloor heating called a **hypocaust**. They usually had barns and other outbuildings for farming. The actual work on the farm would be done by slaves or peasants, who would live somewhere else on the estate.

▼ *A wall painting from Trier. This dates from about AD 150. It is a Roman artist's impression of a villa, with its workers.*

A

SOURCE

The first villas were built in Italy. Many of these were huge houses, run by slaves. As the Roman Empire grew, native people began to copy the Romans and build villas themselves. In northern Gaul, the countryside was full of villas by the end of the Empire. As people became more successful in agriculture, so more villas were built. In north Africa the land was carefully watered (**irrigated**) in order to produce more crops. As they produced more crops, farmers became more wealthy and spent much of their money on rebuilding their homes as villas.

Villas were expensive to build and maintain. For instance, they needed skilled workers from the towns to make things like mosaics. If people were to carry on living in villas, and to build new ones, the Empire needed to be peaceful and prosperous. If the countryside was raided too often, or if trade was reduced, there would not be enough skilled workers, or enough money, to build more villas.

C

SOURCE

A bronze statue from Trier in modern Germany. It shows a villa ploughman in his outdoor clothes.

B

SOURCE

A mosaic of a Roman villa from north Africa. It shows the villa buildings and some of the life of the villa. It dates from about AD 320.

Activities...

1 What are the three key features which most historians agree all villas should have?

2 Sources A and B are the work of artists. How might this affect how useful they are as historical evidence?

3 Look at Sources A and B. Describe the similarities and differences in these pictures of villa buildings.

4 Source A shows a man wearing the same sort of coat as a man in Source C. Does this prove Source C is a reliable source?

3.11 Religious Beliefs

Within the Roman Empire, people believed in many different gods and goddesses. The most important Roman god was Jupiter. There were large temples of Jupiter on the Capitoline hill in Rome, at Doliche in Turkey, and at Baalbek in Syria. Other Roman gods and goddesses included: Neptune, the sea god; Juno, the wife of Jupiter; Mercury, the messenger of the gods; Mars, the war god; Venus, the goddess of love and Minerva, the goddess of wisdom and war.

After Emperor Augustus died in AD 14, emperors themselves began to be worshipped as gods. The emperor was the Chief Priest of the gods. Great services were carried out to please the gods. Animals were sacrificed to the gods of Rome. The government organized and led this worship of the gods.

Many Roman beliefs were based on Greek religious beliefs. Most of these beliefs involved carrying out sacrifices to please the gods. Religious beliefs did not ask people to live good lives. Neither did religion offer people a personal relationship with a god.

B SOURCE

Emperor's order: It is my will that graves and tombs lie undisturbed forever. Respect for those who are dead is most important: no one should disturb them in any way at all. If anyone does, I command that he be executed for tomb robbery.

An order of the Emperor, from the 1st century AD. It was found in Nazareth in modern Israel.

A SOURCE

The Temple of the Roman god Jupiter, in the Roman city of Thugga, in modern Tunisia. It was built in the centre of the city for all to see in AD 166.

C

SOURCE

Underground temple of the 'mystery' god Mithras in Rome.

People throughout the Empire had their own gods and goddesses. They were free to worship them as long as they also worshipped the gods of Rome. Local people often linked their god to the Roman god most similar in character. At Trier (in Germany) the local god Lenus was renamed Mars-Lenus. At Bath (in England) the local god Sul was renamed Sul-Minerva.

By the 2nd century AD, Roman citizens began to be interested in gods from the east of the Empire. One man, Apollonius, travelled to India to find out about other religions. People began to worship Eygptian goddesses like Attis and Cybele. The Persian god Mithras was popular among soldiers. These new religions were called **mystery religions**. People had to pass secret tests to become members of the mystery religions.

D

A carved head from Bath, England. It is probably the British god, Sul. In this carving the god is made to look like the Roman goddess, Minerva.

SOURCE

Activities...

1 a What evidence can you find to show that people linked their local gods to the gods of Rome?
  b How had Roman religious beliefs changed by the 2nd century AD?

2 Look carefully at Sources A and C. Both are temples.
  a In what ways are they different?
  b What does this tell an historian about the two different religions which built these temples?

3 Source B is an official order. Does this mean that all Romans treated the dead with respect?

3.12 The First Christians

In about AD 33, the Jewish preacher and teacher Jesus was executed by the Roman governor Pontius Pilate. Soon the friends of Jesus were spreading the news that God had raised him from the dead. The followers of Jesus' teachings were called **Christians**. Christianity promised people a new relationship with God, instructions on how to live a good life, and life after death. It grew in popularity, often among the poorer citizens. By the 2nd century AD, Christians were being punished by the Roman authorities. This was because they refused to worship the official gods of Rome. Many had already been killed by the Emperor Nero.

Some people distrusted the new religion. They did not understand what Christians believed. At Smyrna (in modern Turkey) and Lyons (in modern France) Christians were killed by mobs. The mobs could kill Christians because Roman law did not protect their religion.

Despite these problems, Christianity continued to attract people. Some emperors allowed it to continue. Others punished the followers of Jesus. However, many people were impressed by the brave way in which Christians stood up to punishment.

A SOURCE

Early Christians praying in the 4th century AD. From a chapel in the villa at Lullingstone, England.

D

SOURCE

Painting of the head of Jesus from the villa at Hinton St Mary, England. It dates from the 4th century AD. The letters behind the head are a Christian sign. They stand for: 'Jesus Christ'.

Activities...

1 a Give reasons why Christianity attracted people.

b Did people's reasons for becoming Christians change over time?

2 a Which of Sources B and C would be most useful, if you were trying to find out why people became Christians?

b Would this source be more, or less, useful than one written by a Christian leader? Explain your answer.

3 a How would an historian be able to identify Source E as having belonged to a Christian?

b Both Sources A and D come from villas. How useful would these sources be as a way of finding out what ordinary people believed? Explain your answer.

They were also impressed by the way in which this new religion changed people's lives. In AD 324, the Emperor Constantine became a Christian. As a result, more and more important people became Christians. The Christian Emperor Theodosius banned other religions. The followers of Jesus were now members of the official religion of the Empire.

E

SOURCE

Pieces of silver from Water Newton, England, 4th century AD.

4.1 The Empire in Crisis

From the 2nd century AD, the Roman Empire was facing problems. After the victory over Carthage it had seemed as if there were no limits to what the Romans could do. By AD 100, this view had changed. The barbarian lands were wild and large. The Roman army could not conquer them all. There had been revolts, against Roman rule, along the rivers Rhine and Danube. At home, rival emperors competed to be in charge of the Empire.

In AD 122, Emperor Hadrian ordered a wall to be built in Britain. It is still called **Hadrian's Wall**. It marked one edge of the Empire. Other boundaries, or **frontiers**, were built in Germany and in Africa. The Romans had realized that there were limits to what they could do. They could not rule the whole world.

Things got worse for the Roman government. The population was falling in the lands around the Mediterranean. This meant there were fewer people to join the army and to pay taxes. The population was falling for a number of reasons. Changes in the weather caused poor harvests. This meant less food for people. Plagues also killed many people.

During the 3rd century AD, trade over long distances began to collapse. It was no longer safe to travel. Law and order was breaking down. Tribes from outside the Empire raided the rich lands of the Romans. These tribes needed more land. They also wanted the luxury goods made by Roman craftspeople. For years they had traded with the Romans. Now the collapse of trade forced their leaders to steal the luxuries they desired.

B SOURCE

In AD 252, the Goths withdrew from the provinces, in return for an annual payment of gold. The ineffectiveness of such desperate measures was almost immediately revealed: not only the frontier regions but the greater part of the western provinces were overrun.

J. Percival, 'The Roman Villa', 1976.

A boat from Nydam in Denmark, 4th century AD. Boats like this may have carried pirates raiding the lands of the Roman Empire.

A SOURCE

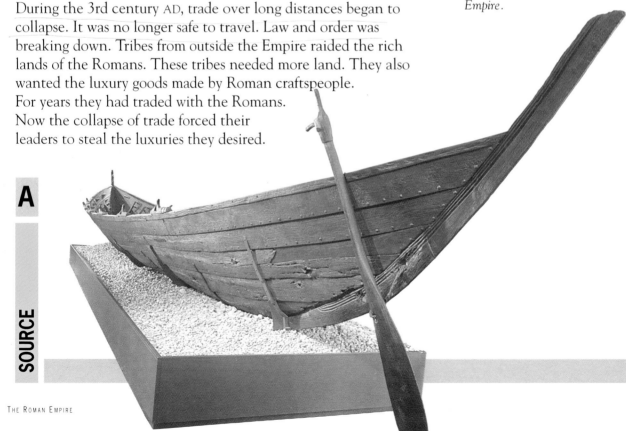

C

The Roman fort of Portus Ardaoni (Portchester) England. This fort was built in about AD 275. It was one of many forts built along both sides of the English Channel. These forts protected the Roman provinces from barbarian pirates (Saxons) from modern Germany and Denmark. They were called the forts of the 'Saxon Shore'.

There were wars in the east with Persia. There were problems all along the frontiers of the Empire. Towns began to decline because there was less to buy and sell.

In AD 251, a German tribe – the **Goths** – killed an emperor. Other tribes invaded the province of Gaul. In AD 270, the province of Dacia was abandoned by Rome. It could no longer be defended against the barbarians. The Empire was beginning to fall apart.

D

Activities...

1 It is the year AD 270. You are a Roman government official. You have to write a report for the Emperor Aurelian. In this report you must explain why the Empire is facing such a crisis. Use the information provided in this Unit to write your report. You may add your own suggestions on the best way to cope with this crisis.

2 a Look at Source B. What did the Romans do to try to keep the barbarians from attacking them?

b Does the writer of Source B think that this was a good or a bad thing to do? How can you tell?

c What other source might support this account that the Romans tried to persuade barbarians to leave the Empire alone? How can you tell?

3 a In what way do the sources agree that the Roman provinces faced attacks from Germany and Denmark?

b Source B is a secondary source. Does that make it more, or less, useful than the other sources?

Pieces of silver from Balline, Northern Ireland. They are stamped with an official Roman mark. They were probably paid to a barbarian tribe to stop them from raiding Roman provinces.

4.2 The Collapse of the Empire

To face the growing problems of the Empire, the army was reorganized. Some troops were kept along the edges of the Empire. Others were made into what is called a **field army**. This could be rushed to wherever there was trouble. However, there were not enough citizens volunteering to join the army any more. People were made to join. This is called **conscription**.

The Emperor Probus (emperor AD 276–82) began to encourage large numbers of friendly barbarians to join the army. They would then fight for Rome against other barbarians. Eventually, by the early years of the 5th century, whole barbarian tribes were allowed to move into the Empire, if they would help to defend it. These soldiers were called **foederati**. Sometimes they could not be trusted.

It was hard to run the huge Empire. In AD 285, Emperor Diocletian split the Empire into two parts. Two emperors (called **Augusti**) would rule. One would be in charge of the west of the Empire, one in charge of the east. In AD 293, each of the Augusti was given a helper, called a **Caesar**. Historians call this the **Tetrarchy** or 'rule of four people'. Even this did not help. There was still rivalry between emperors. The Empire suffered more civil wars as Romans fought Romans.

On top of these problems, prices were going up. This is called **inflation**. Money became worth less and less. In AD 301, Emperor Diocletian tried to stop the prices going up, but he failed.

Within the Empire, the population kept falling. Taxes went up as there were fewer people to pay for its defence. As parts of the Empire were taken by the barbarians, there were even fewer citizens left to tax. Taxes went up again.

In AD 378, more Goths invaded the Empire. They killed Emperor Valens at the **Battle of Adrianople**, in modern Bulgaria. They were being pushed, from behind, by an even fiercer tribe, called the **Huns**. In AD 406, other barbarian tribes invaded Roman Gaul. Some, called **Vandals**, reached as far as Spain and north Africa. Rome was now cut off from its source of grain.

The Roman General Stilicho, who was a barbarian; a Vandal. Like many barbarians, he fought for the Empire against other barbarians. He was executed in AD 408 because he failed to stop the barbarian invasion of Gaul.

Should the Romans, as sensible men, have trusted the defence of Rome to gods who could not defend themselves? The only possible cause of Rome's destruction was this choice of such weak defenders.

The Christian writer Augustine, who lived from AD 354–430.

C **SOURCE**

A mosaic from north Africa, from about AD 490. It shows a Vandal chief riding out from a captured Roman villa.

The Empire was falling apart. Many of the Roman provinces were lost to the barbarians. In AD 410, Alaric, a Goth chief, captured Rome itself. The Goths moved on from Italy, and set up a kingdom in southern Gaul. In AD 476, the last Roman emperor was overthrown by a barbarian chief named Odoacer. The western half of the Roman Empire had collapsed. Only the eastern half was left.

The barbarian invaders of the Roman Empire in the 5th century.

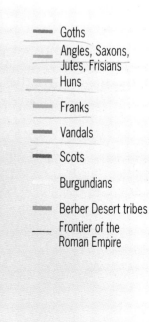

Goths

Angles, Saxons, Jutes, Frisians

Huns

Franks

Vandals

Scots

Burgundians

Berber Desert tribes

Frontier of the Roman Empire

0   1000 km
0   600 miles

Activities...

1 Give one **consequence** for the Roman Empire of each of the following:
   • falling population
   • loss of north Africa.

2 **a** According to the writer of Source B, why did Rome fail to defeat the barbarians?
   b This writer was a Christian and did not believe in the old gods of Rome. How might this have affected his explanation?
   c Using all of the evidence, suggest some reasons of your own why Rome fell.

3 An historian has described the Vandals as the 'mindlessly destructive' enemies of Rome. Using Sources A and C, say whether you agree or disagree with this point of view and why.

4.3 The Collapse of the Empire: Gaul

The Roman province of Gaul was made up of what is now France, Belgium and parts of Germany. As the Roman Empire got weaker, Gaul was invaded by a number of barbarian tribes. We know about these invasions from the writings of Roman historians, church leaders and landowners.

In AD 350, a tribe called the **Franks** crossed the frontier of the river Rhine and invaded north-eastern Gaul. They were looking for new homes. The rich Roman villas offered them a better way of life, if they could capture them. They destroyed 40 towns. They also took land and settled down inside the Empire.

In AD 406, more barbarians invaded Gaul. These tribes included the **Vandals**. They caused terrible destruction in Gaul. Soon Roman Gaul was split up into a number of little kingdoms. Each kingdom was ruled by a barbarian tribe.

The damage to Gaul was made worse by poor farmers who joined in with the barbarian tribes. These farmers were Roman citizens, but they were tired of paying high taxes to the Roman government. They wanted to get rid of their rich landlords and stop paying taxes. These poor farmers, who joined the barbarians, were known as **bacaudae**.

Modern archaeologists and historians are no longer sure that the barbarians were as destructive as some Roman writers tell us. Although the Franks were fierce warriors, they agreed to serve the Roman government. In AD 406, they fought the invading Vandals on behalf of the Roman government.

In time the Franks grew tired of serving the Romans. Under their chief, Clovis, they took more land for themselves. Soon Clovis had united all the Franks under his control.

The Franks were keen to take the best that Gaul had to offer. They wanted to live like wealthy Romans. There is a lot of evidence which suggests that they did not kill the Roman citizens of Gaul. The Franks even learned to speak a kind of Latin (the official language of the western Empire). Clovis himself even became a Christian.

A Death, sorrow, downfall, destruction, fire, unhappiness.

Lines from a poem written in the early 5th century AD. It describes the destruction of Gaul by barbarians.

B SOURCE At the end of the Roman period a number of villas continued to exist and evolved gradually as the centres of villages.

J. Percival writing about Gaul in 'The Roman Villa', 1976.

C SOURCE Leontius [a Roman citizen of Gaul] owns three villas, two near Bordeaux, which produce corn and excellent fishing.

From a poem written in about AD 550.

D SOURCE Before the 5th century, all the grave goods [things buried with the dead] could be described as Roman. During the 6th century there were Frankish weapons and brooches. The natives were just buying whatever happened to be available and fashionable. Not everyone in France became a Frank.

C. Hills, describing a cemetery in Gaul in 'Blood of the British', 1986.

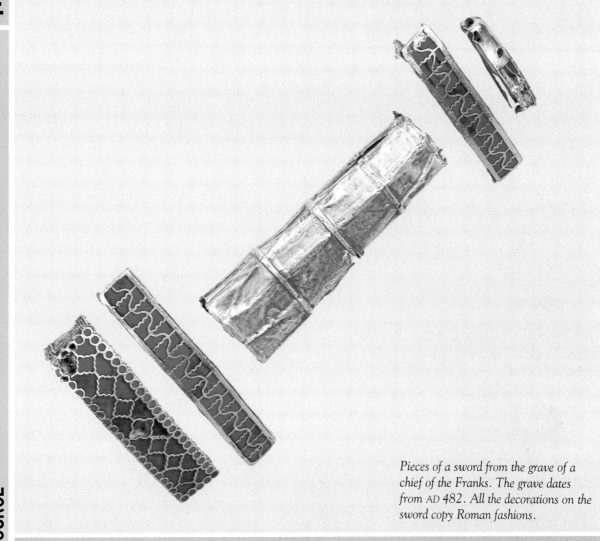

Pieces of a sword from the grave of a chief of the Franks. The grave dates from AD 482. All the decorations on the sword copy Roman fashions.

Activities...

1 Roman pottery stopped being used in Gaul. Does this mean that Roman citizens no longer lived there?

2 a Much of our information about the terrible things done by the barbarians comes from Roman landlords. How might this affect the reliability of these accounts?

b Sources A and C are poems. What problems might an historian face in using poetry as a source of historical information?

3 a Do Sources B and C agree or disagree with the view of events given in Source A? Explain your answer.

b Look at Source E. What could this tell an historian about the Franks' opinion of Roman skills and fashions?

4.4 The Collapse of the Empire: Britain

Britain was part of the western Empire. When Gaul was invaded by barbarians, the Roman government lost control of its provinces in the west. It stopped collecting taxes. After AD 410 no more coins were sent to Britain. Roman towns relied on trade and on taxes. When taxes stopped, the towns lost their reason to exist. The villas changed too. They had nowhere to sell their spare food. They did not need to grow a lot of food in order to sell it to pay taxes any more. They could no longer rely on skilled workers from the towns.

Until fairly recently, historians thought that the barbarian invaders of Britain took over Roman ways of life, as other barbarians did in Gaul, Italy and north Africa. Now it is thought that within about 30 years of AD 410, almost all the things that made Britain 'Roman', vanished. Towns were deserted, villas fell apart, the pottery industry stopped making pots.

As Britain became weaker, it was controlled by barbarians from outside the Empire. These barbarians were called **Angles** and **Saxons**. Before they came to Britain they had lived in modern Denmark, Germany and the Netherlands. Most of these newcomers arrived in Britain after AD 450. A few may have been here before this, as barbarian soldiers in the army. The parts of Britain which eventually came under the control of these barbarians came to be called **England**. These barbarians were the first English.

A SOURCE

◀ *Roman belt buckle worn by soldiers and government officials. This one was worn by an English warrior buried at Mucking, Essex, in about AD 400.*

B SOURCE

All the major towns were destroyed. A number of survivors were caught and killed. Others went to surrender to the enemy. They were fated to be slaves for ever.

Gildas, a British monk, describes what the English did to Britain in about AD 530. Gildas hated the English.

C SOURCE

1 AD 530. In this year Cerdic and Cynric took the Isle of Wight and killed a few men.
2 AD 530. In this year Cerdic and Cynric took the Isle of Wight and killed many men.

An English record of the victory of two English chiefs. The second account was changed later by an English monk.

D SOURCE

We can imagine Anglo-Saxon warriors storming the earthwork camps and stone cities, burning the towns and villas, slaughtering and driving away the Romanised Britons.

G. Trevelyan, 'History of England', 1926.

Historians once thought that the English came to Britain in huge numbers. This was because from the 5th century AD, people in eastern Britain began to be buried with English jewellery and pots and according to English beliefs. Also, the language of the English replaced the language spoken by the Roman Britons. It now seems more likely that the Roman Britons copied the fashions of their new rulers. This was largely because their own industries and ways of life had collapsed.

E SOURCE

The number of Anglo-Saxon migrants to Britain was probably of the order of tens of thousands, as against an indigenous [native] population in the millions. It must mean active participation by large numbers of British in the Anglo-Saxon order of things.

A. Esmonde Cleary, 'The Ending of Roman Britain', 1989.

F SOURCE

A pot made by a Roman British potter, but decorated with a shape and pattern popular with early English barbarians.

G SOURCE

We cannot take it for granted that the Anglo-Saxon conquerors were so destructive as to expel, or exterminate, the Romano-British manpower.

M. Postan, 'The Medieval Society and Economy', 1978.

Activities...

1 The first English arrived in the century that Roman Britain collapsed. Does this mean that they caused this collapse?

2 a Why might there be problems in using Source B to find out how Roman Britain came to an end?
b Look at Source C. How did the monk change the account of the battle?
c Why do you think he did this? Is this important?

3 a Historians often disagree about the events of the past. Use the secondary sources to show how this is true for the end of Roman Britain.
b Why do these differences happen?

4 Look at Sources A and F. What do they tell us about relations between some early English people and Roman British people?

4.5 Survival in the East

In the year AD 330, the Christian Emperor Constantine had a new capital city built for the eastern Empire. He built it on the site of a Greek town, called **Byzantium**. The new city was named after the Emperor himself and called **Constantinople**. It is now Istanbul, in Turkey.

When Rome fell, the eastern part of the Empire survived. Here, the Roman authorities kept control. Most people spoke Greek in this part of the Empire. In the western part, the official language was Latin.

Empress Theodora, Justinian's wife, gives a gift to an Italian church.

A

SOURCE

In the 6th century AD, the eastern Emperor Justinian tried to recapture the lost western Empire. In AD 554, he recaptured Rome and Italy from the barbarians. However, after Justinian died, it was lost again.

In the eastern Empire, the Roman way of life continued. Roman law was still obeyed. The Christian Church was very wealthy and important. Roman ways of planning and building survived. The eastern emperor was powerful. He ruled his Empire using a secret police called the **curiosi**.

In AD 1453, Constantinople was finally captured by the **Muslims**. Until that year, something of Roman life and government had survived in the eastern Empire.

C

SOURCE

By the end of the 6th century Italy was gone again. In eastern Europe too, Justinian had never been successful in dealing with the barbarians. The pressure from behind on these travelling people was too great, and besides they could see great prizes ahead. By Justinian's death a wedge of barbarian peoples separated west and east Rome.

J. Roberts, 'History of the World', 1980.

B

SOURCE

Church of St Sophia, Constantinople. It was built on Justinian's orders and was first used for worship in AD 537.

Activities...

1 Do you think that events worked out as Emperor Justinian intended? Explain your answer.

2 a In the opinion of the writer of Source C, why did Justinian's achievements not last? Explain the reasons using your own words.
b Which of the sources could be used to show that Justinian encouraged Roman skills and ideas to continue in the eastern Empire?

3 a Look at Source A. What impression of the empress do you get from this mosaic?
b Look carefully at Source B. What clues can you find to tell you that this church was captured by Muslims in the 15th century AD?

4.6 The Importance of Rome

Hundreds of years after the end of the Roman Empire, people still remember it. The Romans amazed later peoples by their huge buildings, their careful planning of towns, the way in which they solved problems and their powerful army.

Many of these things were not invented by the Romans. Many of the 'Roman' art, carving and building skills had been inspired by the Etruscans and Greeks whom they conquered. Many of the Roman religious ideas came from Greece and the Middle East. There were not many entirely new Roman inventions.

What amazed later people was how the Romans spread ideas. The Roman Empire made it safe to travel. Skills and ideas spread as never before. Christianity became a 'world' religion because of the Roman Empire.

A

SOURCE

A group of Italian Fascists in the 1920s, dressed as Roman soldiers. At this time Italy was not a powerful country. These Italians were envious of countries, like Britain and France, which had empires of their own. They wished to make Italy powerful once more.

B

SOURCE

Painting of a Roman scene by the French artist Claude. He lived from 1600–1682.

The Romans showed that large areas could be controlled by one government. They also gave lots of different people a common identity. Although they had differences, these people were all members of the Empire.

Many people after the Romans tried to copy Roman planning and building. Many later laws copied the carefully-planned Roman laws. Later rulers tried to control many people, as the Romans had done. Even the Latin language is still used when something is given special importance.

D British 50p coin. The letters 'D. G. REG' are a shortening of the Latin for 'By God's Grace: Queen'.

SOURCE

C The Radcliffe Camera building in Oxford, England. It is the work of the architect James Gibbs, who lived from 1683–1754.

SOURCE

Activities...

1 An **obituary** is a piece of writing about a dead person. It tells us who the person was, what they did, how important they were, how other peoples' lives were changed by that person. Write an obituary for the Roman Empire.

2 **a** Why did the Italians in Source A dress up as Romans?
   b Do you think that Source B is a useful source for finding out what Roman cities really looked like? Explain your answer.

3 **a** The Radcliffe Camera (Source C) has been called the most perfect Roman building in England. What do you think the person who wrote this meant?
   b Look at all the information in this Unit. Describe the ways in which the Romans have influenced the thinking of later people.